50 Shades of Blonde:
Daft things my wife has said

Peter Sowerby

PB Sowerby Books
2017

Copyright © 2016 by Peter Sowerby

All rights reserved. This book or any portion thereof may not be reproduced or used in any manner whatsoever without the express written permission of the publisher except for the use of brief quotations in a book review or scholarly journal.

First Printing: December 2016

ISBN 978-1-326-83023-6

PB Sowerby Books
Lancaster
Lancashire

www.pobz.co.uk

Dedications

This book is dedicated to 2 people:

Firstly my wife, she has said some pretty incredulous things during our time together, some of them common spoonerisms but occasionally an absolute nugget of joy.

After a couple of years I started documenting them and we'd laugh about them in retrospect, eventually we shared them with friends all who had similar experiences with someone we know.

So we decided to put them all together in a book for the world to enjoy.

In the interests of fairness I've allowed my wife a chance to defend herself against each one although I'm convinced some of them are indefensible.

Secondly: The Father of The Blonde, Big Dave who sadly left us all this Christmas but thankfully got to read the proof an hour or so before he died and laughed so much even though it was his own daughter. Both proud and slightly ashamed of her at the same time, but more proud as he always was of both his daughters.

David Williams 1946 - 2016

We hope you enjoy it just as much as he did,

Peter Sowerby

1 .Rain Clouds

Thought Crime

>Whilst on our flight to Las Vegas for our honeymoon, she noted how sunny it was above the clouds and wondered if it ever rained above the clouds.

Defence

>*I still think this is a valid question it is always sunny.*

2 .Speed

Thought Crime

Again whilst flying to our honeymoon destination (it was a long flight) we were talking about how fast the plane was going and I mentioned that jet planes (RAF) were faster as they travelled faster than the speed of sound. Her response:

"That's impossible nothing can travel faster than sound."

I spent the next 30 minutes explaining Mach and sonic booms but couldn't convince her.

Defence

I'm still not convinced & I stand by my response.

3 .Depth

Thought Crime

Whilst looking at watches in duty free I spotted a nice G-Shock that was waterproof to 200m. I showed it the new wife and she said:

"200m that's not very much, so after a few lengths of a 25m swimming pool it stops working?"

Defence

In my defence, it should really say it means depth.

4 .Volume

Thought Crime

Watching TV on a Sunday morning on Channel 4, and on the TV there was a sign language signer in the corner, she said:

"Do they think blind people only watch TV on a Sunday morning?"

Defence

In my defence, it was Sunday morning so I was probably hungover.

5. Agriculture

Thought Crime

> When driving back exhausted from the Great North Run we were passing fields of golden hay along the side of the motorway to which my wife asked:
>
> *"Does hay actually grow or is it always there?"*

Defence

> *We had been up very early and it had been a very long day.*

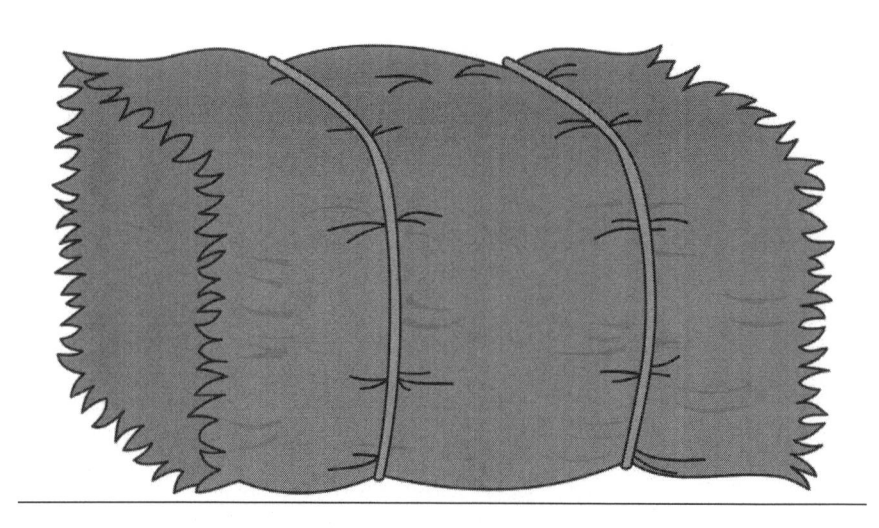

6 .Places

Thought Crime

A bit further down the road we passed a sign saying BP Auckland (Bishop Auckland) to which she asks:

"How big is that petrol station that it needs its own road sign?"

Defence

I stand by my question and still think it's valid.

7. Job Description

Thought Crime

She was feeling under the weather and when being asked a question about what was wrong she replied:

"I am not a Scientician or Magician" …

Defence

I WAS ILL!!!

8. Backed up

Thought Crime

Suffering as my wife does with various aliments this one had me in stitches, she hadn't been able to evacuate for a few days and was in a bit of pain when commenting:

"I need a poo so bad it's backed up all the way to my Fallopian Tubes"

Defence

I was in a lot of pain and certain medical parts of the body do sound very similar.

Female Reproductive System

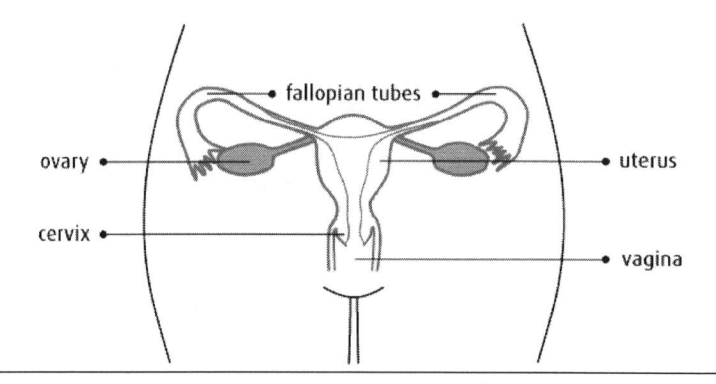

- ovary
- cervix
- fallopian tubes
- uterus
- vagina

9 .Massage

Thought Crime

On a romantic weekend away we booked into the hotel spa for a couples massage, I had to stifle the laughter into my towel when she said to the masseuse:

"Please be careful because I have bad cystitis"

When she meant sciatica.

Defence

And he didn't correct me only telling me afterwards!

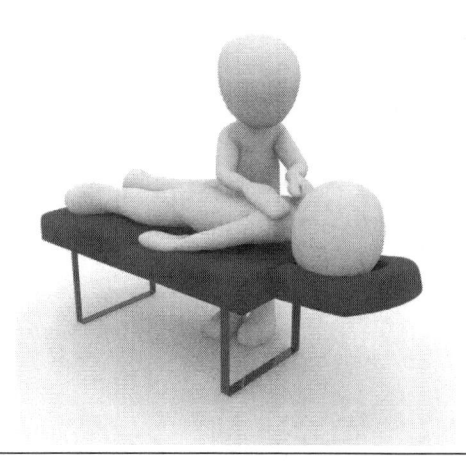

10 . Delirium

Thought Crime

I will start this one off with a bit of a defence for her, she was in unbelievable stomach pain and had been sat on a trolley in A&E for 8 hours!
The doctor asked her if she could have appendicitis and she replied:

"I can't have, only kids can get appendicitis"

She was confused when the doctor said she might have it.

Defence

They don't tell you this in the adverts.

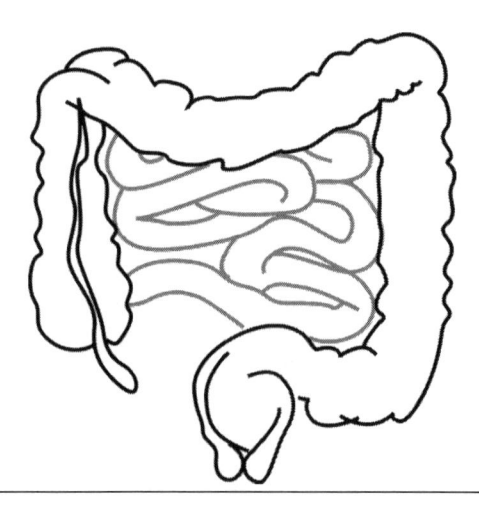

11. Itch

Thought Crime

> My wife's grasp of biology is similar to her grasp on geography!
>
> She used to think the perineum was the back of the knee, Peri meaning behind and neum meaning knee.
>
> She only found out it wasn't when announcing to a room of close friends:
>
> *"Oooh I've got a right itchy perineum"*

Defence

> *No defence your honour.*

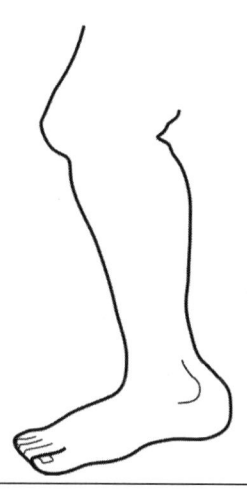

12 .Needles

Thought Crime

Whilst in hospital her fear of needles was brought up when she told people:

"I can't stand this catheter in my right hand"

She meant cannula!!

Defence

The doctor knew what I meant, this must happen a lot.

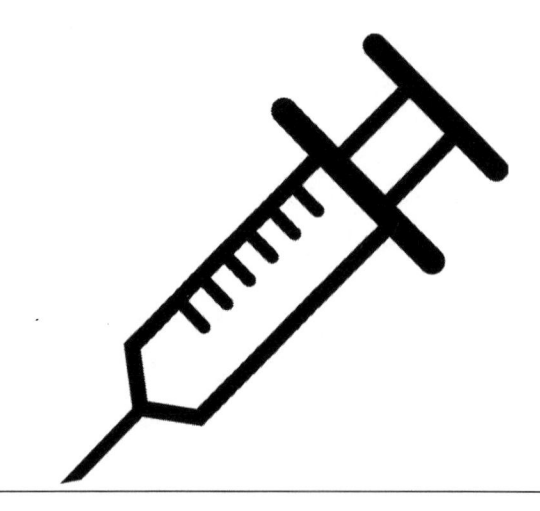

13 .Body Parts

Thought Crime

Keeping on with the health theme she had a bad headache in the front of her head and announced:

"This pain is right in my frontal labia"

Guessing you were going for frontal lobe ☺

Defence

These medical terms again, very confusing.

14. Religion

Thought Crime

> Never try and discuss religion or politics with anyone unless it's Mrs S. then it's hilarious!
>
> *"Don't Jehovah's witnesses castrate their kids?"*

Defence

> *Easy mistake to make.*
>
> I hope not for the kids' sake!

15 .Recipes

Thought Crime

When I met Mrs S, her wine knowledge existed of Red / White or Rose, Coincidently the same as the knowledge of the bar staff in our local!

I expanded her horizons along with Mrs K and introduced her to the variants, but her questions began:

"Which beans do you use to make Chenin Blanc?"

That will be grapes love!!!

Defence

Beans / Grapes ... you say Potayto I say Potarto.

16 .Clean my gutters

Thought Crime

When filling in a medical form for us both, to save me the bother she filled all my items in apart from my height and weight. Thrusting the paperwork towards me she asked me to fill those in and sign it.

Good job I looked as she had put her height as 550cm tall!

I asked what she meant and she said:

"Well I'm 5 foot 5 so that's 550cm isn't it?"

The person receiving the paperwork would have thought I married a giant.

Defence

Aren't feet & metres the same thing?

No!

Well I'm too young to remember feet & inches!

17 .Food for thought

Thought Crime

This one caused a couple of heated discussions!

"Kidney beans can't be a vegetable as they come in a tin!!"

Followed by *"Rice isn't a vegetable its pasta!!"*

Defence

I don't cook a lot from scratch I'm a very busy woman.

18. Anatomy

Thought Crime

    This one had a reverse follow up some time later.

    Thought wine had arms not legs.

    Followed by:

    Thought spectacles had legs not arms.

Defence

    Why is this even a thing? It's just asking to be mixed up & in fairness they are both glasses.

19 .Sight

Thought Crime

This one, again in a nice restaurant, but can't even be blamed on the consumption of alcohol as it was pre drinks!

Whilst looking at the wine list she proclaimed:

"This wine list is in Braille"

No dear that's candle wax on the menu.

Defence

Right! ... Restaurants should really clean their menus.

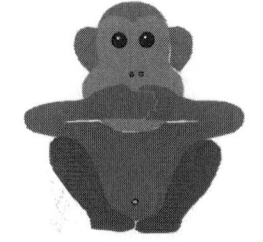

20 .Cake

Thought Crime

An advert for the new Jungle book movie came on the TV but she couldn't understand why a cake maker wrote the children's book. Turned out she thought Rudyard Kipling made exceedingly good cakes!

Defence

They have very similar names I'm sure you would agree.

21. Geography

Thought Crime

> At my last job, I had to work away a lot which meant I got to see some pretty interesting sights like the construction of the new Panama Canal.
>
> When I told her I was off to Argentina with work and it was a 30hr flight she said:
>
> *"How is it 30 hours isn't Argentina in Spain?"*

Defence

> *I will admit I'm not good at geography.*
>
> But you used to travel the world as an Air Stewardess!
>
> *Yes, but I just got on and off the plane at either end I didn't pay any attention.*

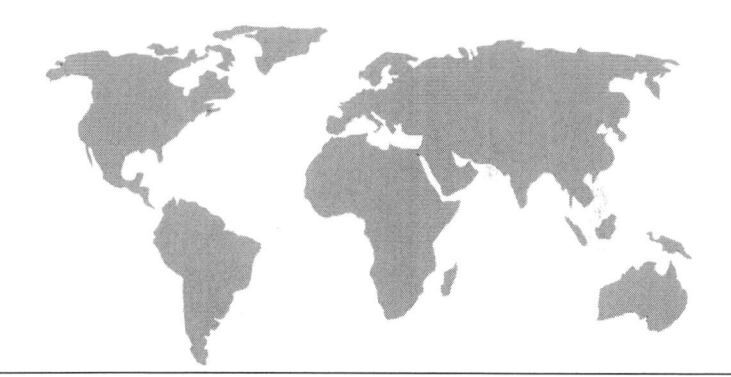

22 .Roaming

Thought Crime

> When getting the cat tag done she asks if we should put the area code on ..... How far is the cat going to wander???

Defence

> *She could have jumped in a car? I didn't want to lose her.*

23 .Pub Crawl

Thought Crime

A friend of hers was doing a sponsored cycle from Lands End to John O Groats.

She though they said the John O' Gaunt a pub in Lancaster.

Defence

So, I focus more on pubs than places, and to be fair Lands End to the John O' Gaunt in Lancaster is still an impressive distance.

24. Pain

Thought Crime

> Whilst on a work trip I got a pretty fancy hire car so I called her to tell her that it even had air conditioned seats which were great for keeping me cool. She asked:
>
> *"Isn't that dangerous having a fan in chairs, won't it cut your balls off?"*

Defence

> *You said the seat was cooling down your man bits.*

25. Wales

Thought Crime

Our TV aerial picks up 2 transmissions, Granada TV and Welsh TV due to our location, so we get 2 BBC ones, 2 Channel 4's etc.

She asked me to record One Born Every Minute and as I was scrolling down the TV guide she said:

"Don't record it on S4C as I can be watching it in Welsh with English subtitles"

Defence

I assumed the Welsh channel would have Welsh dubbing on with English subtitles.

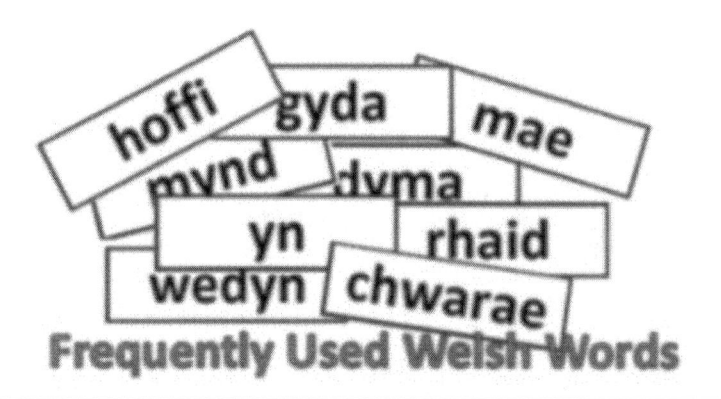

Frequently Used Welsh Words

hoffi · gyda · mae · mynd · dyma · yn · rhaid · wedyn · chwarae

26 .Onomatology

Thought Crime

Only just realised Will.I.Am's name was William.

Ditto for Flo.Rida.

Defence

Who really knew until you saw it written down, be honest?

HELLO My name is **William**

HELLO My name is **Florida**

HELLO My name is **Will.i.am**

HELLO My name is **Flo-Rida**

27. Animals

Thought Crime

Everyone has had a boss quote the following saying at them after a cock up - Never ASSUME it makes an Ass out of YOU & ME!

She thought the saying was:

It makes a knob head out of U & ME.

Defence

I could never get this right until Pete explained it is how you spell it.

28 . The Omen

Thought Crime

When out for lunch with some friends, she spotted a girl running around and playing in front of a mirror in the pub and said:

"Aww look at those twins aren't they cute they even move in the same way".

Defence

The mirror was huge so wasn't obvious.

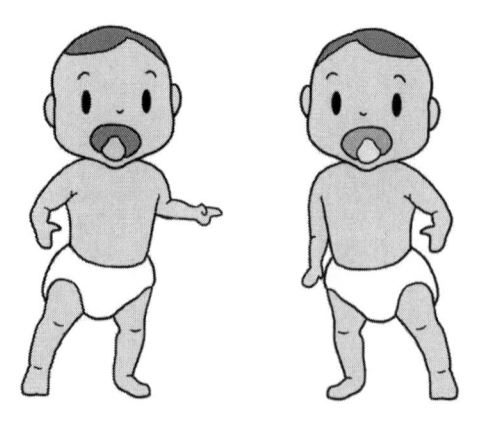

29. Cambodia

Thought Crime

Thought Polpott was the winner of Britain's got Talent.

Defence

It was Paul Potts, I can't be the only person to make that mistake?

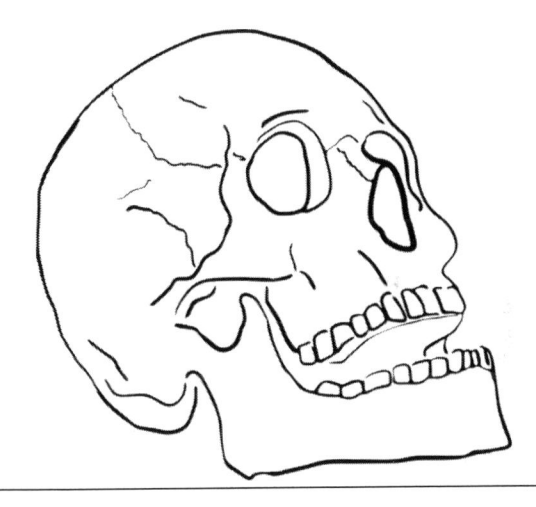

30. Christmas

Thought Crime

Her mother bought her an Advent candle with the dates of Advent on the side and told her to light it for Christmas.

She lit it on the first night and after an hour it had burnt down to the 10th.

"Well this is a rubbish candle it will never last until Christmas Day!"

You're supposed to blow it out when it reaches the next mark.

Defence

Yes, I know this isn't my finest moment.

This still makes us laugh when we're in a church and the priest talks about lighting the massive Easter Candle.

31. New Career

Thought Crime

We hadn't been seeing each other that long and we were round at my parents' house when she came out with this nugget of information.

"I love the word Fudge Packer, I think if I win the lottery I'm going to open a fudge shop just so I can advertise for a fudge packer, no experience needed, and training will be given on the job"

This was said with 100% innocence and she was mortified when I explained the other meaning to her whilst still in the presence of my dad.

Defence

OMG I love fudge & would love to own a shop & I just thought it was a funny job title. Simons face was a picture I was mortified.

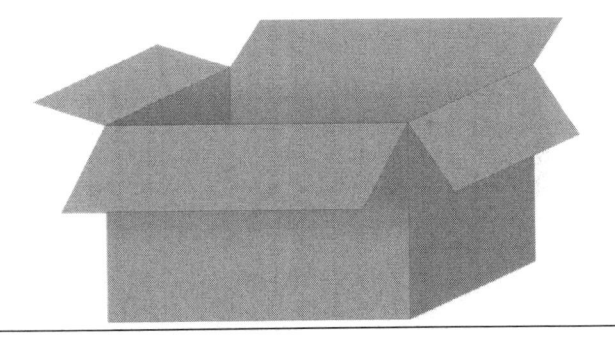

32 .Colour

Thought Crime

At a Sunday school she thought that Moses parted the purple sea.

Defence

Purple looks red in a certain light? & I told you Geography isn't my strongest subject.

33 .DIY

Thought Crime

My sister had purchased a house that required some decoration and had the old-fashioned picture rails & dado rails on the walls. We were sat having a coffee with her and my mother in a well-known coffee shop (that has Wi-Fi that my sister in law "borrows") she asked my sister:

"Are you going to paint your dildo rail when you decorate?"

The shop was packed and a woman sat at the table behind spat her tea all over the window.

Defence

Yes, Sorry Emma for making you sound like a sex crazed woman.

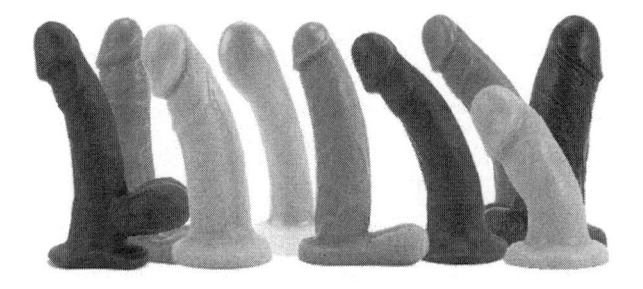

34. Feng Shui

Thought Crime

Upon seeing a display table in a shop with items on she was wondering how much the table would be, as there was no price on it.

I had to stop her asking the sales girl for her own embarrassment.

Defence

It was a lovely table.

35. Dating

Thought Crime

Whilst watching a tea time quiz show (Chase / Pointless / Tipping Point I can't remember which) one of the questions was:

'Willard Libby won a Nobel Prize for discovering what kind of dating?' (The Nobel Prize is a very prestigious scientific award.)

Her answer was ... *"Speed Dating?"*

The actual answer to the science based question was carbon dating.

Defence

I panicked, it was the High Speed Cash Builder Round of The Chase^{TM} and it's the 1st sort of dating I could think of!

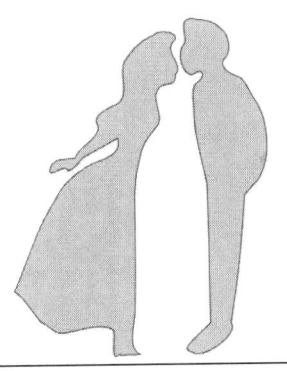

36 .Lost a bet

Thought Crime

When Fernando Torres came on the pitch for the FA cup semi-final with a mask on, I told her it was because he lost a bet and now must dress as Batman for the rest of the season.

To make matters worse she then repeated this to some friends in an attempt to seem like she knew about football!

Defence

You're just mean!

37. Engaging

Thought Crime

Kept calling her own number at work instead of a different branch and wondered why it was always engaged.

Defence

I had a long list of numbers for different offices on my wall & just rang the wrong one. I hadn't been in that office long so didn't know my own number.

Or area code by the look of it!

38 .Accident

Thought Crime

She was involved in a car accident (she was stationary and was rear ended) so her car insurance asked her to fill in the claims form, which she duly did and sent off. Being the thorough person she is she took a copy for her files.

I asked to see the form and she had drawn a diagram of the accident on a car insurance form, but not a plan view of the positioning of the vehicles.

She had drawn a side view complete with stick men.... and the words BANG & OUCH!

Defence

I was asked to draw a picture and I've never had to do it before what was I supposed to think?

39. Dressing up

Thought Crime

>To set the background I have an Uncle called Max and a friend of ours has a child called Max.
>
>Mrs S half overhears a conversation about Max getting dressed up as a spider tomorrow morning for the school Halloween assembly.
>
>*"Why is Uncle Max dressing up as a spider for Halloween? I don't think they'll allow that at work!"*

Defence

>*A simple misunderstanding.*

40. The 90's

Thought Crime

> When singing along to the song by the band 5ive where the lyrics go:
>
> Everybody get up singing,
> 1, 2, 3, 4, Five will make you get down now.
>
> She sang:
>
> *"Everybody get up singing,*
> *Five, 4,3,2,1 Five will make you get down now"*

Defence

> *No defence entered, although I did comment whilst signing them that they didn't make sense.*

41. Good Morning Vietnam

Thought Crime

>We had to leave early one morning for the Manchester 10k run so we were both setting our alarm clocks to prevent us sleeping in when she says:

>*"What is 6am in the 24hr clock?"*

Defence

>*You normally do the alarms!*

42 .Building Work

Thought Crime

When sat in a pub in Manchester after the Manchester 10k (Isotonic lager honest) she noticed a small runner in the middle of the floor.

"Why would they go to the trouble of taking down the entire wall but leaving the doorway carpet gripper in?"

Look up, that's the oche for the dart board.

Defence

Why not just draw a line on the floor to save this confusion?

43. Zoology

Thought Crime

Do chicks turn into ducks??? Erm no that's ducklings!

Defence

A genuine question beautiful.

44. Mixed Wires

Thought Crime

> Whilst I & a good friend were sorting out the electrics in the house with the power off (top tradesman) the wife was dancing a jig in the corner. When we asked her, what was wrong she said:
>
> *"I really need a wee but can I flush the toilet with the electric off?"*

Defence

> *I'm not an electrician.*

45. Neat & Tidy

Thought Crime

I was putting some work together for my boss and needed to make sure it was right, so I was double / triple checking everything. She sent me a text telling me to make sure I went through everything with an anal comb.

Defence

I got mixed up between be anal about everything and go through everything with a fine-tooth comb.

46. Easy Mistake

Thought Crime

Not Mrs S this one but a close friend and still something she would have said!

A friend was moving house and we were putting stuff away when the friend took over and said I need to put the glasses away myself I'm really oral about things like that.

I think you mean anal … but if you get them 2 mixed up you're the Girl for me!!!!

Defence

She has been Blonde on occasions but is currently disguised as a brunette.

47 .Totes Inappropes

Thought Crime

    Sat in a café in town trying to teach my 2 year old to fist bump with explosion (parenting goals 101). She turns to us and says do you want to fist mummy as well?

Defence

    I just thought that's what it meant! ... I have an innocent mind obviously!

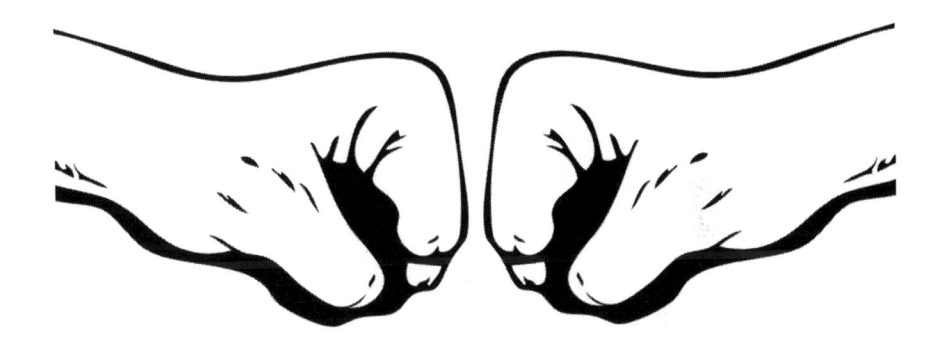

48. Water

Thought Crime

When drinking a bottle of pop I offered a sip to my wife, but as I had been drinking straight from the bottle she said:

I'm not drinking that I don't want any of your splash back!

Backwash maybe but splash back? I was nowhere near the toilet!

Defence

So, I got my words mixed up, probably because you're always talking about your splash back.

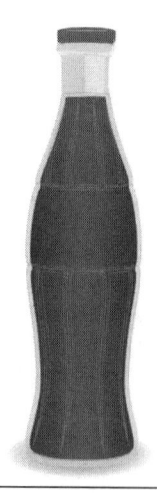

49. Baby Brain

Thought Crime

After the birth of our 1st child she asked me to run upstairs and grab some Nipple clamps.

Luckily I knew she meant Breast Pads!

Defence

Sorry, got you all excited you thought your luck was in!

50 .PC gone mad

Thought Crime

Her computer was running slowly so I said have you emptied the recycle bin on your computer?

"She looked at me blankly and asked why would I tip cardboard and bottles over the computer how's that going to help?"

Defence

We can't all be computer geeks!

Notes

This book was written with the express permission of my wife as it brought us great joy over the years and it was time to share it with more than just our friends.

Thanks for reading I hope you enjoyed it.

As she really is the gift that keeps on giving look out for 50 Shades Blonder later in 2017!

    Pete & The Blonde

Backers

My thanks to the people listed below whose generous contributions made this happen.

Angela Reader, Andrew Webster (AMW Photography), Michelle Holden, Chris Younger, Neil Stevens, Lisa Edmondson, Jake Jackson, Gary Westworth, Kevan Holden, Emma Sowerby, Debbie Sowerby, Simon Sowerby, Clare Benson, Helmut Schindwick, Lindsay Kilifin, Cristina Marsan, Bill Hargenrader, Inglea Asp, Rona Westwell

And most importantly the other half of my world The Blonde.

Printed in Great Britain
by Amazon